THE GREAT PHYSICIAN BRINGS:

HEALING
&
DELIVERANCE
DEVOTIONAL

60 DAYS DECLARING SCRIPTURE

Susan J Perry

Copyright Page

© 2023 Susan J Perry
THE GREAT PHYSICIAN BRINGS:
**Healing & Deliverance Devotion
60 Days Declaring Scripture**

First Printing

This book is inspired by the Holy Spirit, Who teaches us all things.

All Scripture is taken from several versions of the Holy Bible, public domain

Susan J Perry
Edgewater, Florida

Simply This Publishing

Kindle Direct Publishing

Cover Picture © Khunatorn/Adobe Stock

*"GOD said it,
I didn't,
GOD told me to tell you!"*

~ Susan J. Perry ~

3 John 2
Beloved, I wish above all things that
thou mayest prosper and be in health,
even as thy soul prospereth.

CHAPTER INDEX

DEVOTION

Our devotion must always be to Jesus who lived and died for our healing and deliverance exclusively. Today we are free from sin and death by the purging of the Cross of Calvary and the life of our own Jesus Christ! We devote our lives to God the Father; God the Son and empowered by God the Holy Spirit who helps us stay free. Our devotion must be clearly dedicated to this God who is the Blessed Trinity of our lives, making us whole again and again. Our lives in Him may stay that way forever. Jesus offers us salvation and places eternity in our hearts. This is mega good for all who accept the offer. Accept it today; it's a really good offer!

When you are devoted to God you become a child of God and healing and deliverance becomes a natural thing to expect. It is our inheritance as a child of God! Sometimes it's a test of our faith and then you must yell out loud, ***"HELP LORD!"*** And know that He will help you. He loves to heal you and make you whole again! His heart is for you to be more

like Him day by day; healed, delivered and set
free; sanctified for Him.

John 10:10 says this:

*The thief cometh not, but for to steal, and to
kill, and to destroy: I am come that they might
have life, and that they might have it
more abundantly.*

Don't believe the devil today because Jesus
came to give you that abundant life that He has
for you. Take it and be healed! It is our portion
for all of our days, knowing and loving Jesus!
He is our Great Physician!

CENTRAL TRUTH

We are healed and delivered by the blood of the Lamb shed on the cross of Calvary. We are also healed in the name of Jesus. We are going to declare healing & deliverance scriptures in agreement with you as you devote yourself to God for 60 days and are healed day by day. We must know and recognize we are healed by the Word of truth: Faith comes by hearing and hearing by the Word of God! There are 149 healing scriptures in the KJV Bible and I am thinking, clearly healing is a priority with God! He gave His only Son for it (by His stripes we are healed!) Now let's do it! Declare it out loud with us for your healing and deliverance today...

Don't allow fear to come in but embrace God's touch upon your life...

INTRODUCTION

This morning at 4:11 AM on Wednesday, February 9th, 2022 God showed me a picture which looked like a book cover to my understanding. This was an early morning dream state; it was a white sterile background; perhaps a doctor's white lab coat or bare office with a stethoscope hanging loosely in the picture. The stethoscope was dark gray and silver in color. I knew it was for healing and deliverance scriptures for God's people but unfortunately it also came to me that very often folks turn to their doctors first to find the way before they call upon God in prayer. The Bible says to seek God first and His righteousness, in all things and it will be added unto you as in the scripture of Matthew 6:33, example shown here:

Matthew 6:33
But seek first the kingdom of God and his righteousness, and all these things will be added to you.

The results are often much better when seeking God first. This scripture adds years unto people's lives if they follow it. As for me I tried to sleep with this picture in my mind and it didn't work, so I knew God was beckoning me to write. It was His picture to give me for this book. The devotion was already created months ago, and the concept was there but God's picture for the book changed. He is speaking to His people because the world already does this. Go and see the doctor first. This is not God's order of things. Why must you suffer? Because you didn't do Matthew 6:33 first, your suffering may be long. Seek God and He will heal you or seek God and He will direct your steps and send you to the doctors. He does this with me because He knows how I detest going to the doctors hearing worldly instruction and deadly diagnosis spoken over us as the spiritual warfare begins.

Proverbs 16:9
A man's heart deviseth his way: but
the LORD directeth his steps.

Allow God to work on your behalf, give Him your heart and your steps and He will order them; surrender unto Him and He will change your life! Sanctify it and remove all illness and disease forever from you. Now will your body age; will your mind change and grow old? Yes surely it will but Moses died at 120 years, climbed Mt. Nebo and God allowed him to die and bury him. No one knows where he is buried unto this day. Now that surely is submission unto God! Why can't we do that? Surely, we can be more submissive towards God when we seek an intimate, fulfilling relationship between heaven and earth, God responds. Your flesh should be dead and crucified by now to seek God easily in prayer and supplication. (1st)

Now God is not far from you if you but seek Him. He is known as the Great Physician and if you know Him in healing and deliverance, a major issue in life, then you will have no problem getting healed. He knows exactly what you need, He is your Creator from the beginning of time and there is no other. He knows exactly how all of your systems work and collaborate together for the good. Your body must be balanced as He created it. When you break a clock, you take the repair to a clock maker; when the heel comes off of your favorite pair of shoes, you take them to the shoe repair store to have it put back on or replaced. Your body was created and handcrafted by God, why would you go to the doctors' offices first before checking in with the Creator. Doctors are only practicing people studying medicine and the human body. Yes they can put on a band-aide, pass out prescriptions that may help according to your systems but they never heal. Your body has an immune system; a natural repairing system to heal. If you cut your skin, you will see it heal together very soon. It's God's creative systems that HE implemented in your body. My answer to you first of all, is to seek Him and He will give you the steps needed to move forward on your behalf. He loves you; He will help you and improve your life forever if you do it His way. I am a purporter of God's divine healing and deliverance. The Word of God works for all situations and you must learn to trust and depend on our God.

Exodus 15:26
And said, If thou wilt diligently hearken to the voice of the LORD thy God, and wilt do that which is right in his sight, and wilt give ear to his commandments, and keep all his statutes, I will put none of these diseases upon thee, which I have brought upon the Egyptians: for I am the LORD that healeth thee.

All of our devotional books have many things in common but the thread that is most imminent in these is that at the end of each day, a declaration is made aloud declaring the Word of God! It is a great process in your faith walk when you are speaking aloud what God is saying for you. The scripture says:

Romans 10:17
So then faith cometh by hearing, and
hearing by the word of God.

Our LORD has a promise for you as we stand
upon His Word and I want to give it to you
today as we go forward here to see that you are
healed; delivered and set free! Let's chew on
what God has to say:

Deuteronomy 7:15
And the LORD will take away from thee all
sickness, and will put none of the evil diseases
of Egypt, which thou knowest, upon thee; but
will lay them upon all them that hate thee.

Isn't that so good? Is God not a man that He
should lie?

Numbers 23:19
God is not a man, that he should lie; neither
the son of man, that he should repent: hath he
said, and shall he not do it? or hath he spoken,
and shall he not make it good?

We must find God's way and utilize God's
paths that He has set before us and walk on
them. Does your doctor offer this type of
advice: Take two aspirins and I'll call you in the
morning type thing, just remembering those
old funny lines being said by many, years ago?
Doctors have busy lives; busy practices and

they don't much remember you the next time
you appear before them or the symptoms you
presented with either. They come out with this
big folder with your name on it and all you
have suffered with over the years. They ask you
your birth date to see if you still have all your
cognitive facilities about you and thankfully I
still have, I confess that. I guess your birth date
is the ultimate challenge for old-agers! How
about you? How is your faith quotient? Are you
willing to seek God first and watch Him work
or have your fingers done all the walking in the
yellow pages of the physician's section already?
Oh that's right we have internet now and we
can find someone very fast by any search
engine, and all their history. Your choices are
there and God will never go against your will in
any way. Increase your faith this time and give
God your first man to man chat, heart to heart
and see what happens. What is the worst that
could happen? You could go to be with Him?
Huh, that might be the best option ever by far
and not the worse; but to no avail, don't be
foolish but seek God in prayer. He already
knows your need.

Matthew 6:8
Be not ye therefore like unto them:
for your Father knoweth what things ye
have need of, before ye ask him.

Our basis for our clipart is James 5:14-16:

14 *Is any sick among you? let him call for the elders of the church; and let them pray over him, anointing him with oil in the name of the Lord:*

15 *And the prayer of faith shall save the sick, and the Lord shall raise him up; and if he have committed sins, they shall be forgiven him.*

16 *Confess your faults one to another, and pray one for another, that ye may be healed. The effectual fervent prayer of a righteous man availeth much.*

HEALING & DELIVERANCE IS THE CHILDREN'S BREAD!

DAY ONE

Ephesians 6:12
For we wrestle not against flesh and blood,
but against principalities, against powers,
against the rulers of the darkness of this
world, against spiritual wickedness in
high places.

This scripture shows us where the battle lies; it is in the enemies of our soul and not in flesh and blood or mankind, but evil spirits.

Let's declare it aloud today:

"We declare we do not wrestle against mankind but against principalities of darkness, our enemies will not have dominion over us! But GOD will heal us!"

IN JESUS MIGHTY NAME AMEN!

THE LORD'S MERCIES ENDURE FOREVER!

DAY TWO

Psalm 6:2
Have mercy upon me, O LORD; for I am weak:
O LORD, heal me; for my bones
are vexed.

We ask the Lord for mercy upon us as we are weak and some have vexed bones, we ask the Lord to heal us!

Let's declare it aloud today:

"We declare as we are sick and weak, we seek the Lord to heal us! And He will!"

IN JESUS MIGHTY NAME AMEN!

BEGIN TO BELIEVE
BY FAITH YOU HAVE
RECEIVED YOUR HEALING!

DAY THREE

Psalm 30:2
O LORD my God, I cried unto thee, and thou
hast healed me.

When we cry unto the Lord, we expect Him to
hear us and heal us! And our expectation is
high as we pray and declare the Word
of God!

Let's declare it aloud today:

**"We declare as we cry unto the Lord as
the Word says in this Psalm, our God
will heal us! It is inevitable!"**

IN JESUS MIGHTY NAME AMEN!

JESUS SAID ASK ANYTHING IN MY
NAME AND I WILL GIVE IT!

DAY FOUR

Mark 11:24
Therefore I say unto you, What things soever ye desire, when ye pray, believe that ye receive them, and ye shall have them.

It's important that we believe what we are praying for, so healing and deliverance will be received by faith. Come on now; believe for God's healing hand upon you today!

Let's declare it aloud today:

"We declare when we pray, we must believe what we ask for and we will receive by faith in Jesus Christ, our Healer! Our healing is in Him!"

IN JESUS MIGHTY NAME AMEN!

**THE LORD IS MERCIFUL
TO FORGIVE AND HEAL ALL!**

DAY FIVE

Psalm 41:4
I said, LORD, be merciful unto me: heal my
soul; for I have sinned against thee.

We continually ask for mercy from God to heal
us, even when we sin against Him! He
forgives us!

Let's declare it aloud today:

**"We declare our sins before the Lord
and ask Him to forgive us and heal our
souls because He has endless mercy
towards us!"**

IN JESUS MIGHTY NAME AMEN!

**JESUS IS
JEHOVAH ROPHE,
THE LORD GOD OUR HEALER!**

DAY SIX

Luke 5:18-20
18 And, behold, men brought in a bed a man which was taken with a palsy: and they sought means to bring him in, and to lay him before him.

19 And when they could not find by what way they might bring him in because of the multitude, they went upon the housetop, and let him down through the tiling with his couch into the midst before Jesus.

20 And when he saw their faith, he said unto him, Man, thy sins are forgiven thee.

The man with palsy was dropped down through the roof by his friends to Jesus and was healed and forgiven of sin simultaneously, as we can be in salvation as Jesus is not a respecter of persons.

Let's declare it aloud today:

"We declare when we walk in faith, we may be healed and our sins forgiven in salvation simultaneously!"

IN JESUS MIGHTY NAME AMEN!

THERE IS HEALING IN
THE GLORY!

STAY FAR FROM TROUBLE
AND YOUR HEALTH WILL REJOICE!

DAY SEVEN

John 14:1
Let not your heart be troubled: ye believe in
God, believe also in me.

The Word speaks many times 'let not your heart be troubled' and we need a good heart unaffected by the world's woes. We need a clean heart to stay well.

Let's declare it aloud today:

"We declare we will care for our heart and never let trouble near or around it, so we may stay at peace! God forgive us and cleanse our hearts from all hurt and trouble!"

IN JESUS MIGHTY NAME AMEN!

JESUS IS THE WAY, THE TRUTH
AND THE LIFE
WE NEED TO BE HEALED!

DAY EIGHT

1 Peter 2:24
Who his own self bare our sins in his own
body on the tree, that we, being dead to sins,
should live unto
righteousness: by whose stripes ye
were healed

We believe we are healed by the stripes on the
back of Jesus as they beat and killed Him,
dying on the cross for all of us!

Let's declare it aloud today:

**"We declare by the stripes on the back
of Jesus we are healed and set free! His
blood was shed for us!"**

IN JESUS MIGHTY NAME AMEN!

**LAY HANDS ON THE SICK
AND THEY SHALL RECOVER!**

DAY NINE

Psalm 42:11
Why art thou cast down, O my soul? and why
art thou disquieted within me? hope thou in
God: for I shall yet praise him, who is
the health of my countenance, and
my God.

Don't become depressed because of your
sickness because it is God who is our healer!
He is good on His Word!

Let's declare it aloud today:

**"We declare we shall not be cast down
or depressed as we yet praise the Lord
who is the health of our countenance
and our deliverer; He is our God!"**

IN JESUS MIGHTY NAME AMEN!

THE SICK CAME TO JESUS
AND HE HEALED THEM ALL!

DAY TEN

Mark 5:23
And besought him greatly, saying, My little daughter lieth at the point of death: I pray thee, come and lay thy hands on her, that she may be healed; and she shall live.

Jesus often laid hands on the sick and they recovered and some He only spoke to and they were healed and delivered, Selah! His power is everlasting!

Let's declare it aloud today:

"We declare when we lay hands on the sick as Jesus did, they will recover and become set free! Be healed today!"

IN JESUS MIGHTY NAME AMEN!

PRAYER AND ANOINTING OIL WORKS IN AN ACT OF FAITH!

DAY ELEVEN

James 5:14
Is any sick among you? let him call for
the elders of the church; and let them pray
over him, anointing him with oil in the name
of the Lord:

We are healed as others pray for us such as
James speaks of the elders in the church to
anoint and pray in the name of the Lord! This
operation works!

Let's declare it aloud today:

**"We declare when we get sick, we call
upon the elders of the church and they
will anoint us and pray over us in the
name of the Lord and we will
be healed!"**

IN JESUS MIGHTY NAME AMEN!

JESUS STILL HEALS TODAY!

DAY TWELVE

Jeremiah 17:14
Heal me, O LORD, and I shall be healed; save
me, and I shall be saved: for thou art
my praise.

Even in your praise healing comes as you faithfully seek God! He wants you healed so you may be more effective for the Kingdom of God!

Let's declare it aloud today:

"We declare when we cry out to the Lord: "Heal me oh Lord and save me O Lord" during our praise, it shall be done!""

IN JESUS MIGHTY NAME AMEN!

JESUS WANTS TO HEAL YOU!

DAY THIRTEEN

Hebrews 13:8
Jesus Christ the same yesterday, and to day,
and for ever.

The Lord never changes; He is the same as yesterday, today and forever! We know Him today as Healer!

Let's declare it aloud today:

"We declare Jesus is the same as yesterday, today and forever and He still heals! We are healed!"

IN JESUS MIGHTY NAME AMEN!

**THE LORD HEALS BY
THE LAYING ON OF YOUR HANDS!**

DAY FOURTEEN

Psalm 107:20
He sent his word, and healed them, and
delivered them from their destructions.

This scripture is very effective in healing and
deliverance, one of my personal favorites! It
will work on your behalf too!

Let's declare it aloud today:

**"We declare He sent His Word and
healed them, and delivered them from
their destruction! We are healed!"**

IN JESUS MIGHTY NAME AMEN!

FAITH IS AN IMPORTANT QUOTIENT IN YOUR HEALING!

DAY FIFTEEN

Hebrews 11:1
Now faith is the substance of things hoped for,
the evidence of things not seen.

Faith is important in every aspect of our walk with Jesus and although it is unseen, we continue to hope for it especially in our healing and deliverance! Stay in faith and you will see the best results!

Let's declare it aloud today:

"We declare we have faith enough, although unseen, for healing and deliverance!"

IN JESUS MIGHTY NAME AMEN!

DEVOTION UNTO GOD
LEADS TO HEALING & DELIVERANCE!

DAY SIXTEEN

Isaiah 57:18
I have seen his ways, and will heal him: I will lead him also, and restore comforts unto him and to his mourners.

The Lord heals us because we are His; He also leads and comforts us! Believe on Him!

Let's declare it aloud today:

"We declare God has seen our ways and will heal us, lead us and comfort us because we belong to Him! We are His children, and He never fails!"

IN JESUS MIGHTY NAME AMEN!

THE LORD APPOINTS AND ANOINTS
WHOM HE HAS CHOSEN!

DAY SEVENTEEN

Luke 4:18
The Spirit of the Lord is upon me, because he hath anointed me to preach the gospel to the poor; he hath sent me to heal the brokenhearted, to preach deliverance to the captives, and recovering of sight to the blind, to set at liberty them that are bruised,

Allow the Spirit of the Lord to heal and deliver the people as Isaiah spoke about in prophecy in his time! There are many elements in our healings and the Word of God will help us get there!

Let's declare it aloud today:

"We declare the Spirit of the Lord is upon us, because He has anointed us to preach the gospel, and sent us to heal the broken-hearted and deliver the captives and give them liberty! Let's go now!"

IN JESUS MIGHTY NAME AMEN!

**JESUS IS THE
ONLY REDEEMER!**

DAY EIGHTEEN

Isaiah 10:27
And it shall come to pass in that day, that his burden shall be taken away from off thy shoulder, and his yoke from off thy neck, and the yoke shall be destroyed because of the anointing

The anointing of the Spirit breaks the yoke of bondage from off of thy neck and destroys it completely! Let's let Him work on us!

Let's declare it aloud today:

"We declare we have that yoke-destroying, demon- delivering kind of anointing upon us given straight from Heaven and now we can all be set free too!"

IN JESUS MIGHTY NAME AMEN!

LAUGH WITH THE KING,
IT WILL BRING HEALTH
TO YOUR BONES!

DAY NINETEEN

Proverbs 17:22
A merry heart doeth good like a medicine:
but a broken spirit drieth the bones.

HAHAHAHA! Get some laughter and joy down
in your heart because it is like good medicine!
Live a full life filled with God's joy!

Let's declare it aloud today:

**"We declare a merry heart does good
for our health, its like a medicine but
sorrow will dry up your bones and
your spirit will become brittle and old!
Today we are moving forward in joy!"**

IN JESUS MIGHTY NAME AMEN!

THE TWINS OF HEALING
& DELIVERANCE,
FREE YOU BY THE FIRE
OF THE HOLY SPIRIT!

DAY TWENTY

Psalm 103:3
Who forgiveth all thine iniquities; who healeth all thy diseases;

God does it all; He forgives and heals us! He makes us whole as we believe on Him!

Let's declare it aloud today:

"We declare it is the Lord who forgives us and heals us always! He is so merciful and loving!"

IN JESUS MIGHTY NAME AMEN!

**IN THE FEAR
OF THE LORD,
HEALING & DELIVERANCE
WILL COME!**

DAY TWENTY-ONE

Malachi 4:2
But unto you that fear my name shall the Sun
of righteousness arise with healing in his
wings; and ye shall go forth, and grow up as
calves of the stall.

The Lord is the Sun of righteousness and we
are healed under His wings, and we shall go
forth stronger than the young calves we see in
their stalls! Jesus can do this for us!

Let's declare it aloud today:

**"We declare as we fear the name of the
Sun of righteousness we shall be healed
under His wings and grow up strong as
young calves in the stall!"**

IN JESUS MIGHTY NAME AMEN!

THE PRAYER OF FAITH
STILL WORKS!

DAY TWENTY-TWO

James 5:16
Confess your faults one to another, and pray one for another, that ye may be healed. The effectual fervent prayer of a righteous man availeth much.

There is so much that works in prayer; healing is only one of them! Be fervent in prayer and it shall become effectual for you and whoever you are praying for!

Let's declare it aloud today:

"We declare if we confess our faults one to another and pray we will be healed because the effectual fervent prayer of a righteous man avails much before the Throne of God!"

IN JESUS MIGHTY NAME AMEN!

SALVATION IN JESUS
WILL HEAL YOU!

DAY TWENTY-THREE

James 5:15
And the prayer of faith shall save the sick, and the Lord shall raise him up; and if he have committed sins, they shall be forgiven him.

God hears our prayers, as we pray in faith the sick will be healed; the sin-sick shall be forgiven! The body-sick will be healed!

Let's declare it aloud today:

"We declare the prayer of faith shall heal the sick and God will forgive the sin-sick as well!"

IN JESUS MIGHTY NAME AMEN!

THE LORD HEARS THE CRIES OF HIS PEOPLE!

DAY TWENTY-FOUR

Numbers 12:13
And Moses cried unto the LORD,
saying, Heal her now, O God, I beseech thee.

Moses cried unto the Lord for healing for his
sister Miriam who had spoken evil about him,
as can we! We need to cry out to God for
other's healing as well as our own!

Let's declare it aloud today:

**"We declare if you heard Moses Lord as
he cried out to heal Miriam, you can
hear us and heal all of our family too!
We believe on You!"**

IN JESUS MIGHTY NAME AMEN!

THE DAY OF HEALING IS TODAY!

DAY TWENTY-FIVE

Isaiah 57:19
I create the fruit of the lips; Peace, peace to
him that is far off, and to him that is near,
saith the LORD; and I will heal him.

The Lord creates all things, peace is only one
fruit of the Spirit but very beautiful as He
creates the fruit of our lips, those near to Him
He will surely heal.

Let's declare it aloud today:

**"We declare the Lord creates the fruit of
the lips and His peace which He gives
us and those near Him, He will
heal us!"**

IN JESUS MIGHTY NAME AMEN!

CLEANSE OUR HEARTS
OH GOD!

DAY TWENTY-SIX

Luke 9:42
And as he was yet a coming, the devil threw him down, and tare him. And Jesus rebuked the unclean spirit, and healed the child, and delivered him again to his father.

Father sent Jesus to heal and deliver them all! He knows all about it! Call upon His holy, healing name today!

Let's declare it aloud today:

"We declare our Father in Heaven sent Jesus to heal and deliver all, we call upon His holy name today!"

IN JESUS MIGHTY NAME AMEN!

THERE IS NO HIDING PLACE
FOR THE DEVIL,
HE MUST COME OUT!

DAY TWENTY-SEVEN

Psalm 32:7
Thou art my hiding place; thou shalt preserve
me from trouble; thou shalt compass me
about with songs of deliverance. Selah.

We can hide in God, but the devil cannot and
the Lord will sing songs of deliverance over you
and me! Let's listen intently for His
melodious voice!

Let's declare it aloud today:

**"We declare our hiding place is in the
Lord and He will compass us about and
sing songs of deliverance over us and
we will be set free!"**

IN JESUS MIGHTY NAME AMEN!

JESUS NEVER CHANGES!

DAY TWENTY-EIGHT

Matthew 4:23
And Jesus went about all Galilee, teaching in their synagogues, and preaching the gospel of the kingdom, and healing all manner of sickness and all manner of disease among the people.

Jesus went about healing them all and you are included in this now! Add your name to that list! You are healed!

Let's declare it aloud today:

"We declare Jesus healed them ALL and He will heal you and me too, no doubt here!"

IN JESUS MIGHTY NAME AMEN!

**OUR LORD JESUS
LOVES YOU!**

DAY TWENTY-NINE

Jeremiah 29:11
"For I know the plans I have for you," declares
the LORD, "plans to prosper you and not to
harm you, plans to give you hope and
a future."

God has a good plan for all us, did you know
that? This is one of my favorite verses here
because my husband and I were married under
it. We trust God to care for us always! He will
heal and deliver us when necessary too!

Let's declare it aloud today:

**"We declare God has perfect plans for
us and we will trust Him implicitly! Our
healing and deliverance is included!"**

IN JESUS MIGHTY NAME AMEN!

**KEEP YOUR WORDS KIND
TO OTHERS!**

DAY THIRTY

Proverbs 16:24
Pleasant words are as an honeycomb, sweet to the soul, and health to the bones.

Saying a kind word or giving a nice thought to someone can be healing to them when broken. Give them a big hug too!

Let's declare it aloud today:

"We declare that our pleasant words are sweet to the soul, and very healthy as we speak them to others! Our healing will come!"

IN JESUS MIGHTY NAME AMEN!

A HEART IS A GOOD THING
TO PROTECT!

DAY THIRTY-ONE

Ecclesiastes 3:3
A time to kill, and a time to heal; a time to
break down, and a time to build up;

There is a timing in God and we must
recognize this and be healed in His timing and
in His way! Submit to God our Father and
be healed!

Let's declare it aloud today:

"We declare the timing of God is upon
us and we will be healed!"

IN JESUS MIGHTY NAME AMEN!

WALK AND TALK WITH JESUS, YOU WILL BE HEALED!

DAY THIRTY-TWO

Romans 3:24
Being justified freely by his grace through the
redemption that is in Christ Jesus:

When we stay in Christ, we stay healed and
delivered because He has redeemed us! We are
protected in His presence!

Let's declare it aloud today:

**"We declare when we stay in Christ we
are redeemed from sickness and disease
and we are healed!"**

IN JESUS MIGHTY NAME AMEN!

THE HOLY SPIRIT WILL
CAUSE YOU TO BE HEALED!

DAY THIRTY-THREE

1 Corinthians 12:9
To another faith by the same Spirit; to
another the gifts of healing by the same Spirit;

We are given gifts by the Lord to minister with and one such gift is healing! This is all done through the Holy Spirit!

Let's declare it aloud today:

"We declare by faith we have the gift of healing by the Holy Spirit on the inside of us, to minister! We are so thankful!"

IN JESUS MIGHTY NAME AMEN!

**JESUS IS ALWAYS THE WAY;
ALWAYS THE TRUTH AND
ALWAYS THE LIFE!**

DAY THIRTY-FOUR

1 Corinthians 12:31
But covet earnestly the best gifts: and yet
shew I unto you a more excellent way

Desire the best gifts from God and He will
show us the excellent way! (His way) It is in
His excellent will that we will be healed!

Let's declare it aloud today:

**"We declare God has given us the best
gifts and He will show us a more
excellent way and we will be healed!"**

IN JESUS MIGHTY NAME AMEN!

OUR REDEEMER LIVES!

DAY THIRTY-FIVE

Exodus 15:26
And said, If thou wilt diligently hearken to the
voice of the LORD thy God, and wilt do that
which is right in his sight, and wilt give ear to
his commandments, and keep all his statutes, I
will put none of these diseases upon thee,
which I have brought upon the Egyptians: for
I am the LORD that healeth thee.

The Lord declares here that only He will heal
us and we must believe on Him for it!

Let's declare it aloud today:

**"We declare that we are the healed of
the Lord, forevermore!"**

IN JESUS MIGHTY NAME AMEN!

**AT THE CROSS WE
LAY DOWN OUR SICKNESS!**

DAY THIRTY-SIX

Job 19:25
*For I know that my redeemer liveth, and that
he shall stand at the latter day upon the earth:*

I know my redeemer lives it says in this
scripture and He redeemed us from sin,
sickness and disease, and death, hell and the
grave altogether!

Let's declare it aloud today:

**"We declare our redeemer lives and He
died for our sickness and disease; our
sin and death were released at
the cross!"**

IN JESUS MIGHTY NAME AMEN!

IT'S IN THE PRESENCE
OF GOD
WHERE WE ARE
HEALED & DELIVERED!

DAY THIRTY-SEVEN

Psalm 16:11
Thou wilt shew me the path of life: in thy
presence is fulness of joy; at thy right hand
there are pleasures for evermore.

Find joy in the Holy Ghost and you will find
healing and deliverance in God's presence
which brings joy and pleasure! It is our portion
as children of God! Claim your inheritance!

Let's declare it aloud today:

**"We declare there is much joy in God's
presence and at His presence there are
pleasures forevermore that we have not
discovered yet, healing is only one! And
we claim it today!"**

IN JESUS MIGHTY NAME AMEN!

**WE ARE HEALED
IN THE NAME OF JESUS!**

DAY THIRTY-EIGHT

Proverbs 23:11
For their redeemer is mighty; he shall plead
their cause with thee.

Our Redeemer Jesus will plead our cause
before our Father in Heaven for He is seated at
His right-hand interceding on our behalf for
every need!

Let's declare it aloud today:

**"We declare Jesus is our Redeemer and
He will plead our cause before Father in
Heaven and we will be set free from
sickness or disease!"**

IN JESUS MIGHTY NAME AMEN!

**THE LORD WILL NEVER LEAVE YOU
NOR FORSAKE YOU
BUT IS HEALING YOU NOW!**

DAY THIRTY NINE

John 5:13
But the one who was healed did not know who it was, for Jesus had withdrawn, a multitude being in that place.

Sometimes we don't recognize Jesus as our healer, because you cannot see Him always; but don't forget HE is your healer and no one else!

Let's declare it aloud today:

"We declare Jesus is our healer even when we can't see Him or hear Him, we know He is there!"

IN JESUS MIGHTY NAME AMEN!

JESUS HEALED THEM ALL!

DAY FORTY

Luke 17:14-15
14 So when He saw them, He said to
them, "Go, show yourselves to the
priests." And so it was that as they went, they
were cleansed.

15 And one of them, when he saw that he was
healed, returned, and with a loud
voice glorified God,

Jesus healed the ten lepers and only one
turned back to thank Him! Let us be that one!

Let's declare it aloud today:

"We declare we will always be thankful
for the healing Jesus gives no matter
the seriousness of the illness, or the test
and trial it becomes!"

IN JESUS MIGHTY NAME AMEN!

**ALWAYS BE THANKFUL
TO JESUS
FOR YOUR HEALING
& DELIVERANCE!**

DAY FORTY-ONE

1 Thessalonians 5:18
In every thing give thanks: for this is the will
of God in Christ Jesus concerning you.

Stay thankful to the Lord for everything and
you will be in right standing with Him! You
will be healed as you thank Him in advance!

Let's declare it aloud today:

**"We declare we shall be thankful for
everything in Christ Jesus because He
is so good to us!"**

IN JESUS MIGHTY NAME AMEN!

WE ARE HEALED
BY THE BLOOD OF JESUS!

DAY FORTY-TWO

Isaiah 53:5
But he was wounded for our transgressions,
he was bruised for our iniquities: the
chastisement of our peace was upon him; and
with his stripes we are healed.

We have depended on Jesus on the cross to be
healed because of the stripes put upon His
back during those horrendous beatings He
took willingly! His death was not in vain but
for all of us!

Let's declare it aloud today:

**"We declare we are healed by the blood
of Jesus shed on the Cross!"**

IN JESUS MIGHTY NAME AMEN!

EVEN THE DEVILS
KNOW JESUS!

DAY FORTY-THREE

Mark 1:34
And he healed many that were sick of divers diseases, and cast out many devils; and suffered not the devils to speak, because they knew him.

Key phrase here is: because they knew him. Do you know Jesus today? Get healed and delivered by His mighty hand!

Let's declare it aloud:

"We declare we know the Lord Jesus Christ and we are healed because of Him!"

IN JESUS MIGHTY NAME AMEN!

**EVERY KNEE SHALL BOW,
EVERY TONGUE CONFESS
THAT JESUS CHRIST IS LORD!**

DAY FORTY-FOUR

Acts 3:16
And his name through faith in his name hath made this man strong, whom ye see and know: yea, the faith which is by him hath given him this perfect soundness in the presence of you all.

In the name of Jesus you shall be healed; signed, sealed and delivered by the hand of the Lord! His name is all-powerful!

Let's declare it aloud today:

"We declare we are healed and delivered by the name of Jesus, the name above every name!

IN JESUS MIGHTY NAME AMEN!

THE NAME OF JESUS IS
HIGH AND LIFTED UP!

DAY FORTY-FIVE

Philippians 2:9
Wherefore God also hath highly exalted him,
and given him a name which
is above every name:

Every thing is done in Jesus name and we as believers in Christ rely heavily on His name! Father has given us permission to use it in power and authority!

Let's declare it aloud today:

"We declare as God's children we rely on the name of Jesus; the name above every other name! This name can move mountains!"

IN JESUS MIGHTY NAME AMEN!

WHO ELSE MAY WE GO TO, BUT TO THE LORD?

DAY FORTY-SIX

Psalm 46:1
God is our refuge and strength, a very present
help in trouble

Where else do we go when we are sick or
troubled? We go to the Lord and seek
Him diligently!

Let's declare it aloud today:

**"We declare our strength and healing
comes from the Lord when we seek
Him, for He is our refuge!**

IN JESUS MIGHTY NAME AMEN!

GIVE PRAISES UNTO GOD
FOR YOUR HEALING IN ADVANCE!

DAY FORTY-SEVEN

Psalm 47:1
O clap your hands, all ye people; shout unto God with the voice of triumph

Oh get your healing and deliverance in the praises of your God as you clap your hands and shout, triumph will come! Healing will come! Hallelujah!

Let's declare it aloud today:

"We declare our healing and deliverance comes when we praise the Lord, clap our hands and shout hallelujah, there is triumph!"

IN JESUS MIGHTY NAME AMEN!

HOW GREAT IS OUR GOD
TO HEAL US!

DAY FORTY-EIGHT

Psalm 48:1
Great is the LORD, and greatly to be praised in
the city of our God, in the mountain of
his holiness.

So much happens in the praises of our God and
healing comes as we extol His holy name!

Let's declare it aloud today:

**"We declare we are healed because
great is our Lord, and greatly to be
praised in the city of our God and the
mountain of His holiness!"**

IN JESUS MIGHTY NAME AMEN!

**WE MUST BEGIN TO STOP TALKING,
AND GIVE EAR TO THE LORD'S WORDS,
THEY ARE IMPORTANT!**

DAY FORTY-NINE

Psalm 49:1
Hear this, all ye people; give ear, all ye
inhabitants of the world:

Give ear to what the Lord says to you! We
praise the name of Jesus for our healing
and deliverance!

Let's declare it aloud today:

**"We declare we will give ear to the Lord
Jesus and give importance to His words
and we will be healed and delivered!"**

IN JESUS MIGHTY NAME AMEN!

THE LORD LOVES US
NO MATTER OUR CONDITION!

DAY FIFTY

Psalm 147:3
He healeth the broken in heart, and bindeth up their wounds.

God heals those with broken hearts and broken spirits due to loss of any kind because He has mercy and compassion upon us. There are many kinds of healings a person needs and Father knows about them all!

Let's declare it aloud today:

"We declare the Lord heals us when we are broken hearted and our souls are stricken by loss because of His mercy and compassion!"

IN JESUS MIGHTY NAME AMEN!

GOD'S MERCY IS NEW EVERY DAY!

DAY FIFTY-ONE

Psalm 51:1
Have mercy upon me, O God, according to thy
lovingkindness: according unto the multitude
of thy tender mercies blot out
my transgressions.

God's mercy is great towards us and when we
are in sin, sickness and disease may come upon
us, but He will clean us up in salvation
and love!

Let's declare it aloud today:

**"We declare God's mercy is great
beyond our own sin as we call upon
Him to clean us up in salvation
and love!"**

IN JESUS MIGHTY NAME AMEN!

WE ARE NOT ANYTHING
THE WORLD SAYS,
BUT MORE THAN CONQUERORS!

DAY FIFTY-TWO

Psalm 43:5
Why art thou cast down, O my soul? and why art thou disquieted within me? hope in God: for I shall yet praise him, who is the health of my countenance, and my God.

Why are you so depressed and angry? Our hope is in God and as we yet praise Him there is health coming to our countenance!

Let's declare it aloud today:

"We declare we are not depressed; possessed; oppressed but as we yet praise our God we shall see health coming back to our countenance!"

IN JESUS MIGHTY NAME AMEN!

THE FOOLISH
DO NOT KNOW OUR GOD!

DAY FIFTY-THREE

Psalm 53:1
The fool hath said in his heart, There is no
God. Corrupt are they, and have done
abominable iniquity: there is none that
doeth good.

Let us not be fools unto God but walk upright
and say, *"We are healed and delivered!"*

Let's declare it aloud today:

**"We declare the fool has said in his
heart, "There is no God!" But we
declare there is a great God who heals
and delivers us!"**

IN JESUS MIGHTY NAME AMEN!

HALLELUJAH
WE ARE HEALED!

DAY FIFTY-FOUR

Psalm 54:1
Save me, O God, by thy name, and judge me
by thy strength.

God will save us, heal us, deliver and judge us
by His strength, thankfully!

Let's declare it aloud today:

**"We declare the Lord will do all things
by His name and in His strength and
not man's!"**

IN JESUS MIGHTY NAME AMEN!

HOW MANY KNOW
THE LORD DOES NOT
HIDE HIMSELF FROM US?

DAY FIFTY-FIVE

Psalm 55:1
Give ear to my prayer, O God; and hide not thyself from my supplication.

Our prayers and supplications go before God and He will hear them and heal us! It is His will for us!

Let's declare it aloud today:

"We declare give ear to our prayer O God, and hear our supplications so those we pray for may be healed!"

IN JESUS MIGHTY NAME AMEN!

CAST OUT DEVILS
AND SEND THEM TO
THE BOTTOMLESS PIT!

DAY FIFTY-SIX

Luke 8:36
They also which saw it told them by
what means he that was possessed of the
devils was healed.

Possession of devils in someone needs Jesus to heal, deliver and set free! Come out now!

Let's declare it aloud today:

"We declare those who are possessed by devils must be healed and delivered by Jesus to cast them out! Shout GO OUT NOW!"

IN JESUS MIGHTY NAME AMEN!

THE LIGHT DELIVERS
THE DARKNESS!

DAY FIFTY-SEVEN

John 8:12
Then spake Jesus again unto them, saying, I
am the light of the world: he that followeth me
shall not walk in darkness, but shall
have the light of life.

Follow Jesus who is light and there shall be no
darkness around you and you will be delivered!
Darkness cannot stay in the Light!

Let's declare it aloud today:

**"We declare the light delivers the
darkness as we follow Jesus as He
spoke to us here!"**

IN JESUS MIGHTY NAME AMEN!

DECLARE TRUTH TODAY
OVER YOURSELVES!

DAY FIFTY-EIGHT

Psalm 118:17
I shall not die, but live, and declare the works
of the LORD.

We must declare life over ourselves if we are to live and not die! GOD works in His Word; He watches over it to be performed.

Let's declare it aloud today:

"We declare we will not die but live to declare the mighty works of the Lord"

IN JESUS MIGHTY NAME AMEN!

JESUS ASKED, "WHO TOUCHED ME?" HAVE YOU TOUCHED JESUS TODAY?

DAY FIFTY-NINE

Luke 8:47
And when the woman saw that she was not hid, she came trembling, and falling down before him, she declared unto him before all the people for what cause she had touched him, and how she was healed immediately.

This woman with the issue of blood was healed (after 12 years) as she was determined to be so; because she grabbed a hold of the hem of the garment of Jesus and was healed immediately!

Let's declare it aloud today:

"We declare as we get desperate and grab the hem of His garment; Jesus will give us the miracle of healing too! Our God is great!"

IN JESUS MIGHTY NAME AMEN!

JESUS CAN BE TOUCHED,
AND HE WILL TOUCH YOU,
AND YOU WILL BE HEALED!

DAY SIXTY

Luke 8:45
And Jesus said, Who touched me? When all denied, Peter and they that were with him said, Master, the multitude throng thee and press thee, and sayest thou, Who touched me?

Jesus in a crowd of many people asked the question, *"Who touched me?"* And by scriptures we know who touched Him but have you touched Him today in your time alone? Have you asked Him for your healing yet? Simple as that is to ask!

Let's declare it aloud today:

"We declare when we touch Jesus He will heal us in our desperation and sickness, because we are His, let's touch Him today!"

IN JESUS MIGHTY NAME AMEN!

SALVATION PRAYER

Let's pray together...

Lord Jesus, I confess that I am a sinner and in need of salvation. I believe that You came to earth to seek and to save people who are lost in their sins, and I believe that You died on the cross as the substitute for my sins.

I believe that You took the punishment that I deserved for the sins that I have committed, and forgave me all my sins. I believe that You died for me and that You rose again from the dead, and that whoever believes in You will not perish but have everlasting life.

I trust in You and I place my faith in You. Thank You for dying for me, forgiving my sins, making me clean and covering me in Your own perfect righteousness. Thank You for all that You have done for me.

I receive You into my life as my Saviour and I choose to follow You and serve You all my life. Thank You for hearing my prayer, Amen.

CONCLUSION

Jesus is forever the way to be healed in mind, body and spirit! There really is no other way if you truly give way to the Word of God. Yes we go to doctors, hospitals and therapists but the best they can do is put a band-aide on it or prescribe medicines to aid in your healing. Jesus is the optimum healer and never a man. He desires for us to be made whole. All else is a lie. Do not be deceived because they are only practicing and God is the Healer, or Great Physician or Balm of Gilead, He is all that we proclaim here today!

Matthew 15:28
Then Jesus answered and said unto her, O woman, great is thy faith: be it unto thee even as thou wilt. And her daughter was made whole from that very hour.

And we hope you will get something out of this book. We toiled diligently on your behalf because we know healing is our portion in the

Kingdom of God. We hope we have been a helping hand as you declare these scriptures out loud to hear the Word in your spirit man.

John 1:1
In the beginning was the Word, and the Word was with God, and the Word was God.

AUTHOR'S CORNER

Susan J Perry born January 12, 1952 in Niskayuna, New York and resided in Schenectady, NY most of her early life. She graduated from Schalmont High School in Rotterdam, NY in 1970. She was saved to Jesus in the fall of 1998 in Houston, Texas where she lived for twenty-five years. She now lives and writes in Edgewater, Florida for sixteen years. She is married to John R Perry and they have 4 children in their blended marriage and 6 grandchildren who live all over the United States of America. They visit as much as they can.

She loves and serves her Lord Jesus Christ knowing only by His Spirit does she write and create page by page. Pure inspiration is so beautiful as the mornings run into nights and nights into mornings as she taps the keyboard on one finger quickly and as accurately as possible. She and her husband now publish books in *Simply This Publishing* and are having a great time doing so. Life is good for both of them. They give God all the praise, the honor and the glory for His loving ways. God is so good!

They have just started on children's books which are a new avenue for them and they hope it will work. They pray and ask God to direct their paths, and the funny thing is He does. God is in the blessing business and today is no different, God never changes, thankfully so.

They attend Edgewater Church of God in Edgewater, Florida with Bishop William T White and they love it there hearing the truth of God's Word. They are active in the church and are very thankful that they now serve locally, helping out as they are able.

Susan and her husband are ordained by Dr Frank and Karen Sumrall of Sumrall Global Ministries of Bristol, Virginia. Their life's call is in the Ministry of Helps to go into churches and help the Pastors wherever help is needed. They have an Aaron and Hur ministry of holding up the arms of the Pastors as they have need.

Exodus 17:12
But Moses' hands became heavy; so they took a stone and put it under him, and he sat on it. And Aaron and Hur supported his hands, one on one side, and the other on the other side; and his hands were steady until the going down of the sun.

Susan speaks at women's groups in churches when invited. She is now teaching one of her books in Sunday night classes in her own church: "Lessons In Deliverance." What a time they are having too! They often find themselves in Clearwater or Dunedin, Florida on the west coast while they live on the east coast and love every minute of it. They take their books and have a product table to set up wherever they go. She and her husband go where the Lord sends them and they are glad to do it. God always provides.

Psalm 100:2
Serve the LORD with gladness; come before his presence with joy.

CONTACT THE PERRYS

1 Corinthians 14:3
But he who prophesies speaks edification and exhortation and comfort to men

All available on www.Amazon.com
Kindle Direct Publishing
Simply This Publishing
John & Susan Perry
Edgewater, Florida

Contact info:

Susan J Perry, Email:
susiebqt987p@yahoo.com
& Facebook; Simply This Publishing

John R Perry, Email: jperry8@bellsouth.net

ALL BOOKS AVAILABLE ON AMAZON.COM

Books can also be ordered through bookstores and big box stores if that is your preference. There is always a way.

PERRY'S BOOK SHELF

The Samaritan Woman Testifies
Kindle only: $9.95

A Stone's Throw Away: A Woman Testifies
Paperback: $12.95 Kindle: $6.99

The Persistent Widow Testifies
Paperback: $12.95 Kindle: $6.99

The Woman Presenting the Alabaster Box Testifies
Paperback: $12.95 Kindle: $6.99

Hidden in the Cleft of the Rock: A Woman Testifies
Paperback: $12.95 Kindle: $6.99

Simply This: The World's Greatest Message
Paperback: $5.95 Kindle: $3.99

Preach It Sister Girl!
Paperback: $9.95 Kindle: $5.99

Daughters of Inheritance Testify
Paperback: $12.95 Kindle: $6.99

**ASK for WISDOM: The Safe Harbor
of God**
Hardcover $15.95 Paperback: $9.95
Kindle: $5.99

**Great Holes in Your Pockets:
Recovering All!**
Paperback: $9.95 Kindle $5.99

This Project is Called: HONOR
Hardcover $15.95 Paperback: $12.95
Kindle: $5.99

Our Experiences With ANGELS
Paperback $9.95 Kindle $5.99

I AM A DUCK!
Paperback $9.95 Kindle $5.95

The Double-Dip Blessings
Paperback $9.95 Kindle $5.99

**The Woman Touching the Hem of His
Garment Testifies**
Paperback $12.95 Kindle $6.99

It's Never Too Late To Pray
Paperback $5.95 Kindle $2.99

This is the Anemic Church
Paperback $9.95 Kindle $5.99

There is a Witness!
Paperback $9.95 Kindle $5.99

Heal Them ALL! The Children's Portion
Paperback $7.95 Kindle $3.99

Ye Shall Serve God Upon This Mountain!
Paperback $9.95 Kindle $5.99

Thanksgiving Is Best!
Paperback $7.95 Kindle $3.99

The ABC'S of Perry
Paperback for kids $12.95

LOVE is Surely the Way
Paperback $7.95 Kindle $3.99

Lessons In Deliverance
Paperback $12.95 Kindle $6.99
Cancel Cancer: And The Effects Thereof
Paperback $9.95 Kindle $5.99

Royalty BELONGS To The Believer!
Paperback $9.95 Kindle $5.99

"Just When Did This Happen?"
Paperback $9.95 Kindle $5.99

I Declare Over You in Jesus Name
Paperback $5.95 Kindle $3.99

**With Blessing & Favour
Will You Compass Me About!**
Paperback $9.95 Kindle $5.99

**Going Down The Barker Road
Missing...**
Paperback $9.95 Kindle $5.99

**Deception of Man: Sin Lies At The
Door**
Hard cover $15.95 Paperback $12.95
Kindle $6.99

Beautiful Things: Out Of The Dust
Paperback $9.95 Kindle $5.99

**In My Weakness God is Strong:
Declarations of Strength: 60 Days**
Paperback $15.95 Kindle $8.99

**The Year of 2022: A Miraculous Work!
60 Day Devotional**
Hardcover $15.95 Paperback $12.95
Kindle $6.99

Love Endures Devotional:
60 Day Devotional
Paperback $12.95 Kindle $6.99

TRAUMA: The Doors Opened to a
Unique Spirit
Hardcover $15.95 Paperback $12.95
Kindle $6.99

Baking A Cake With GOD'S Ingredients
Hardcover $15.95 Paperback $12.95
Kindle $8.99

The Holy Spirit Is Our Comforter
Paperback $12.95 Kindle $6.99

Be Anxious For Nothing But Pray
About Everything!
Paperback $12.95 Kindle $6.99

Pastor's Declaration Devotional
Paperback $12.95 Kindle $6.99

Because I Asked For Wisdom
Devotional
Paperback $12.95 Kindle $6.99

Our Devotional For America: In The
Year of Our Lord
Hardcover $15.95 Paperback $12.95
Kindle $6.99

**The ABC'S of GOD:
Knowing God More**
Paperback $5.95

**Psalm 139 is Mine!
The Presence and the Power of God**
Paperback $5.95

Your Benefit Package In God
Paperback $5.95

**Devotions In Prayer Unto God!
60 Day Devotional**
Paperback $9.95 Kindle $5.99

**Blessing & Favor Devotional:
60 Days Of Overflowing Devotion**
Paperback $12.95 Kindle $6.99

**Christmas: When They Saw The STAR
They Rejoiced With Exceeding Great
Joy! 30 Day Devotional**
Paperback $9.95 Kindle $5.99

**The Year of 2023 In Devotion:
The Year of the Shepherd**
Hardcover $15.95 Paperback $12.95
Kindle $6.99

Devotions In The 7 Spirits of God
Paperback $12.95 Kindle $6.99

His Name is Wonderful!
60 Days of Devotion
Paperback $12.95 Kindle $6.99

Cry Out Unto God!
Paperback $5.95

THE GREAT PHYSICIAN BRINGS:
Healing & Deliverance Devotion
60 Days Declaring Scripture
Paperback $12.95 Kindle $6.99

RESOURCES

Free black & white clipart

Wikipedia

Bible Gateway online

Various Bible translations as needed

Holy Spirit indwelling in inspiration and wisdom

Edgewater Church of God, perfect example

You tube Instrumental Music to write by

Various online Dictionaries

www.Amazon.com

No copyright infringement intended here

The Joy of the Lord is my Strength!

WE MUST KNOW THESE THINGS
BY GOD'S PERSEPECTIVE
AND NOT OUR OWN!